A TROOP OF GORILLAS

KELLEY BARTH

childsworld.com

The Child's World
childsworld.com

Published by The Child's World®
800-599-READ • www.childsworld.com

Photography Credits
page 1: ©MikeLane45/Getty Images; page 1: ©GlobalP/Getty Images; page 2: ©Anastasiia Verych/Shutterstock; page 6: ©dikkyoesin1/Getty Images; page 10: ©Tom Applegate/Getty Images; page 13: ©guenterguni/Getty Images; page 14: ©wlablack/Getty Images; page 17: ©Buena Vista Images/Getty Images;page 19: ©hpboerman/ Getty Images

ISBN Information
9781503884977 (Reinforced Library Binding)
9781503885905 (Portable Document Format)
9781503886544 (Online Multi-user eBook)
9781503887183 (Electronic Publication)

LCCN 2023937377

Printed in the United States of America

BRINGING THE WORLD TO YOUNG READERS 1968

Kelley Barth is a former children's librarian who loves connecting with young people over stories and books. When she isn't busy writing, Kelley enjoys reading, hiking, crafting, and exploring national parks. She lives in Minnesota with her husband and dog.

TABLE OF CONTENTS

CHAPTER 1

Meet the Troop 4

CHAPTER 2

All in the Family 8

CHAPTER 3

Who's in Charge? 12

CHAPTER 4

What Makes Troops Unique? 18

CHAPTER 5

Why Troops Matter 20

Wonder More . . . 21

Pound Sounds . . . 22

Glossary . . . 23

Find Out More . . . 24

Index . . . 24

CHAPTER 1

Meet the Troop

It is morning in the **tropical rainforest**. Patches of sunlight shine through the thick, leafy branches. Suddenly, there is a rustling sound. A group of gorillas comes into a forest clearing. It is time for breakfast!

Gorillas live in tropical forests throughout central Africa. There are four different types of gorillas. The western lowland gorilla is the smallest and most common. Eastern lowland gorillas have larger hands and shorter noses. They are also the largest. Mountain gorillas have thicker fur to keep them warm. There are very few Cross River gorillas in the wild.

But all types of gorillas have something in common. They live, work, and play in groups. A group of gorillas is called a troop.

AFRICA
Atlantic
Ocean
Indian
Ocean
KEY
Where
gorillas live

Older male gorillas are easy to spot because of the patch of silver fur on their backs.

Gorillas are very social animals. They live together in troops of up to 30 gorillas. Most troops have around 10 gorillas. One or two members of the troop are males. The rest are females.

Every gorilla in a troop has an important role. The leader of the troop is called a **silverback**. A silverback is an older, large male. He keeps the troop safe. He also makes troop decisions. Blackbacks are younger male gorillas. Sometimes a troop has a **matriarch**. This is usually the oldest female that has had the most babies. The matriarch is not the leader, but she gets a lot of respect from the rest of the troop.

CHAPTER 2

All in the Family

Gorilla mothers carry their babies everywhere for the first few months. Soon, babies grow strong enough to ride on their mother's back. Baby gorillas have strong hands and feet. They grip the hair on their mothers' backs so they won't fall off. Babies nurse, or drink their mother's milk, for two or three years.

When baby gorillas are four or five months old they can walk on their own. They find plants and fruits to chew on. Soon they learn to eat foods such as bamboo shoots and insects. Baby gorillas are very playful. They wrestle, run, and climb trees. After four years, young gorillas are **independent**. They are fully grown after eight to ten years. When a gorilla is fully grown, it leaves the troop it was born into and starts a troop of its own.

Gorilla Size Comparison

Gorillas are between 49 and 69 inches (125–175 centimeters) tall when standing up. Female gorillas weigh between 154 and 250 pounds (70–113 kilograms). Males are heavier. They weigh between 298 and 400 pounds (135–180 kg).

The average human is between 5 feet 4 inches and 5 feet 9 inches (162–175 cm) tall.

A baby gorilla stays close to its mother for the first few years of its life.

SWEET DREAMS

The gorillas in a troop sleep around 12 hours each night. Adult gorillas often nap during the day. The baby gorillas in the troop climb and play on the adults as they nap. Every night, gorillas make a nest for sleeping. Nests are made from leaves and branches. A nest is hardly ever used twice. Young gorillas sleep in a nest with their mother until she has a new baby. Scientists who study gorillas count nests to see how many gorillas are in a troop.

From the day it is born, a baby gorilla is part of the troop. The other gorillas in the troop sniff and touch the baby to get to know it. Younger female gorillas and other gorilla moms all help raise the baby. They hold and play with the baby so the mom can have a break. Father gorillas also help care for their babies. They hug and play with them. Sometimes they even carry them on their backs. If a mother gorilla becomes sick or dies, the father often takes over its care. Another nursing mother in the troop might even adopt the baby and feed it as her own.

CHAPTER 3

Who's in Charge?

All male gorillas develop a patch of silver hair on their backs. This happens when they are around 12 years old. But only one male becomes the true silverback, or troop leader. The silverback is usually the oldest, largest, strongest male in the troop. He protects the other troop members. He keeps the peace and helps settle conflicts. Silverbacks are usually peaceful. But if an intruder bothers the troop, a silverback will fight to keep his troop safe.

Silverbacks get the best spots in the troop for eating and sleeping.

Groups of young male gorillas often travel, eat, and sleep together.

Silverbacks **mate** with the females in the troop. He does this to pass on his **genes** and have a big family. When his sons get older, they leave or get kicked out of the troop. The silverback does not want to compete for mating rights. These young males often form **bachelor** troops with other male gorillas until they are old enough to start their own family. Gorillas rarely live on their own. There is safety in numbers!

Male gorillas follow in their father's footsteps over time. When a male gorilla is around 12 years old, he finds one or more female gorillas. They mate and start their own troop.

There are no female leaders in a troop. But there is a **hierarchy** among the females. When a female is pregnant, she moves up in importance. The other females in the troop **defer** to her. The silverback gives her more attention. A pregnant gorilla also gets the best feeding spots. She is allowed to eat and sleep close to the silverback.

Female gorillas that have had more babies have a higher **rank**. The more babies born in a troop over time, the more **stable** the troop will be. Females that have good relationships with the other members of the troop also get more respect. And although a baby gorilla has to wait a long time to become a leader, a gorilla infant gets lots of attention from the troop. All of the troop's members take responsibility for a baby gorilla's safety.

A gorilla that is expecting a baby gets special attention from the rest of the troop.

CHAPTER 4

What Makes Troops Unique?

Gorillas are the largest **primate**. Humans are primates, too. Both gorillas and humans grip things with their hands. They use objects as tools. They live in family groups and have unique personalities.

Like humans, gorilla troops communicate in many ways. Gorillas can make over 20 unique sounds. Happy gorillas laugh or grunt. Worried gorillas scream. Baby gorillas hum while they eat. And like human families, gorilla troops have unique signals and looks that other troops might not understand. Gorillas are usually shy. But they are fierce if they need to protect themselves. A gorilla that feels threatened or upset pounds its chest loudly. This shows the gorilla's strength to predators or intruders.

Gorillas have a lot to say! They communicate with each other in many ways.

NO TWO ALIKE

Most everyone knows that no two humans have the same fingerprint. This is another thing humans and gorillas have in common. But it is a gorilla's "nose print" that sets it apart! Like humans, gorillas have unique face shapes and features. Their noses are especially unique, and scientists use noses to tell members of a troop apart. One gorilla researcher made nose drawings in her journal for each gorilla she encountered. Today, scientists take photos of troop members' noses. This allows them to research the habits, behaviors, and health of the troop.

CHAPTER 5

Why Troops Matter

Gorilla troops are important. Sadly, all four kinds of gorillas are **endangered**. Some gorilla troops live on protected lands. Virunga National Park is the oldest national park in Africa. It is home to hundreds of mountain gorillas. The park rangers at Virunga work hard to protect the gorillas.

Gorilla troops keep the environment healthy. They spread seeds of the plants they eat. This helps more plants grow. Other animals rely on these plants for food. Saving gorillas will also help many other animals. Thankfully, people are working hard to help gorilla troops. They are spreading the word about these important animals. Hopefully, this work will make it possible for gorilla troops to live and work together for a long time.

Wonder More

Wondering about New Information

What new information did you learn about gorilla troops? Write down three new facts that you learned. Did this information surprise you? Why or why not?

Wondering How It Matters

How are gorilla troops similar to human families or communities? List three things gorilla troops and human families have in common.

Wondering Why

Gorillas are endangered. Why do you think gorillas are endangered? What can you do to help endangered animals?

Ways to Keep Wondering

After reading this book, what questions do you have about gorilla troops? What can you do to learn more about them?

Pound Sounds

Silverbacks are famous for the loud sound that comes from pounding on their chests. Try an experiment to find out which materials will give the best booming echo just like a gorilla.

What You Need:

- Objects from around your house. Some ideas to try: a pillow, an empty bucket, this book, a chair, a metal pot. Anything will work. Get creative.
- Pencil and paper

Steps to Take:

1. Gather the items you are curious about. Try to have at least four different items.
2. One at a time, try lightly pounding on each item with your hands. Avoid objects that are fragile or that have sharp edges that might hurt your hands.
3. Write down your results. Which item was the loudest when you pounded on it? Did it echo? Was the sound low or high?
4. Feel free to try the experiment again with four new items. Make some predictions about what type of sound each item will have.

Glossary

bachelor (BATCH-uh-lur) A bachelor is a male human or animal that does not have a partner.

defer (dee-FUR) To defer is to show preference to someone or something else.

endangered (en-DAYN-jurd) Endangered animals, plants, or other living things are at risk of dying out.

genes (JEENS) Genes are the patterns of DNA that are passed from parent to offspring.

hierarchy (HY-ur-ar-kee) A hierarchy is a system that ranks a group or family based on importance, strength, or power.

independent (in-duh-PEN-dunt) Independent animals are able to look after themselves.

mate (MAYT) When animals mate, they join together to produce offspring.

matriarch (MAY-tree-ark) A matriarch is the female leader of a family, group, or organization.

primate (PRY-mayt) A primate is a type of mammal that has hands and feet that can grasp.

rank (RANK) Rank is an animal or person's place in a hierarchy.

silverback (SIL-vur-bak) A silverback is a dominant male gorilla with gray fur on his back.

stable (STAY-bul) A stable group is usually not weak and does not fall apart easily.

tropical rainforest (TRAH-pik-ul RAYN-for-ust) A tropical rainforest is a wooded area with many tall trees that gets a lot of rain every year.

Find Out More

In the Library

Applegate, Katherine. *Ivan: A Gorilla's True Story.* Boston, MA: Clarion Books/Houghton Mifflin Harcourt, 2020.

Gibbons, Gail. *Gorillas.* New York, NY: Holiday House, 2021.

Smalls, June. *He Leads: Mountain Gorilla, the Gentle Giant.* Reedley, CA: Familius LLC, 2022.

On the Web

Visit our website for links about gorilla troops:
childsworld.com/links

Note to Parents, Caregivers, Teachers, and Librarians: We routinely verify our web links to make sure they are safe and active sites. So encourage your readers to check them out!

Index

Cross River gorilla, 4

eastern lowland gorillas, 4

primate(s), 18

silverback, 7, 12–13, 15–16

Virunga National Park, 20

western lowland gorilla, 4